THE GLOW-IN-THE-DARK BOOK OF

ANIMAL SKELETONS

By **REGINA KAHNEY** Illustrated by **CHRISTOPHER SANTORO**

*Our thanks to Dr. Nancy B. Simmons, mammalian evolutionary
biologist at the American Museum of Natural History, New York City,
for her expertise and enthusiasm.*

Random House New York

Library of Congress Cataloging-in-Publication Data
Kahney, Regina.
   The glow-in-the-dark book of animal skeletons / by Regina Kahney ; illustrated by Christopher Santoro.
      p.   cm.
   Summary: Depicts and explains the skeletal structure and movement of such animals as the cheetah, bat, cobra, and human. The skeleton illustrations glow in the dark.
   ISBN 0-679-81080-3
   1. Skeleton—Juvenile literature. 2. Glow-in-the-dark books—Specimens. [1. Skeleton. 2. Glow-in-the-dark books. 3. Toy and movable books.] I. Santoro, Christopher, ill. II. Title.
QL821.K28   1992   599'.0471—dc20   91-3810
                                                          Manufactured in Taiwan   10 9 8 7 6 5 4 3 2 1

Human being

(*Homo sapiens sapiens*; worldwide, except extreme polar and tropical regions)

You belong to the animal group known as vertebrates. That means you have a backbone, or spine—a long column of small bones (vertebrae) that runs down your back and supports your entire body. Touch the middle of your back to feel this column of bones. It sets you apart from insects, worms, and jellyfish, which are called invertebrates.

Backboned animals come in many shapes and sizes, depending on where they live and how they survive. But the shape of your skeleton, and the way your bones work together, allow you to move in ways not possible for most other animals.

You are a mammal—a warm-blooded animal that breathes air and has hair or fur—and you are the only mammal built to walk comfortably on two legs. That is because your pelvis (hipbone) and backbone are in a straight line with your legs, unlike the same bones in other animals, which lie at an angle to the legs.

Your feet are also made for walking. Long and wide, they carry the weight of your entire body. Your toes are short and do not move as freely as your fingers, but that's okay, because human toes are meant for balance, not for gripping a tree branch like a bird's claws or a monkey's feet.

Because you can walk upright, your arms and hands are free for other tasks. Your fingers are very flexible, and your "opposable" thumb can touch (or be "opposite" to) each of the other fingertips, so your hands work like precision tools.

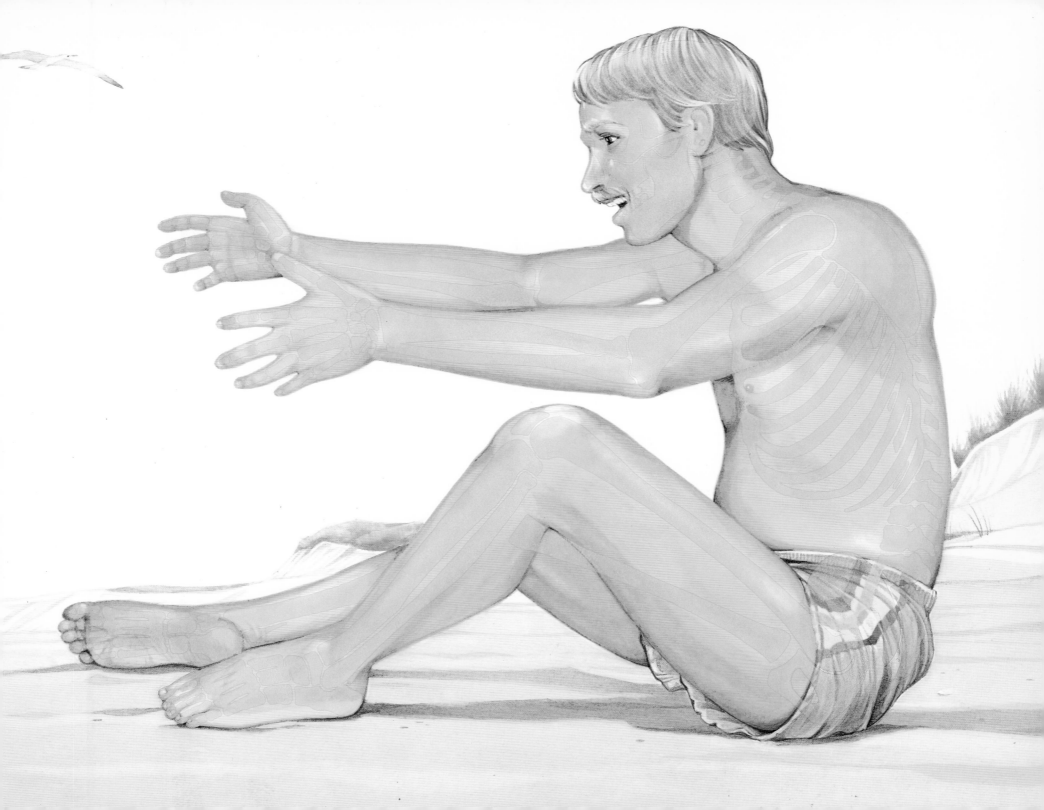

Chimpanzee
(*Pan troglodytes*; Africa)

The chimp is an expert climber because its feet act like an extra pair of hands. Its big toe is opposable, unlike your big toe, and can be spread widely from the other toes, so the chimp can wrap its foot around each branch. And the chimpanzee's arms are longer than its legs, so it can reach far and swing from branch to branch.

Chimpanzees are "knuckle walkers"—they walk on the soles of their feet and the knuckles of their hands. They can shamble along upright if they have to, but not for long. Their pelvis lies at a slight angle to the legs, and their knees do not straighten, as yours do.

Chimpanzee hands are a lot like yours. With their flexible fingers and opposable thumbs, chimps can strip the leaves off a twig and use the twig to "fish" for termites. Chimps are the only other creatures besides humans that actually *make* tools.

6

Black-handed spider monkey

(Ateles geoffroyi; Central America)

The undisputed acrobat of the Central American rain forest is the spider monkey. It lives high up in the trees and rarely comes down to the jungle floor. Its long tail is common to many tree-dwelling monkeys.

The spider monkey's tail is "prehensile," which means it can grasp things the way a human hand can. The tip of the tail curls around and is as nimble as a set of fingers. The tail is an extension of the backbone, but it is one and a half times longer than the monkey's body—perfect for gathering food that cannot be reached with the arms. It is so strong that it can support the monkey's entire weight.

Usually, a spider monkey's fingers are permanently curved, which enables the monkey to get a firm grasp on each tree branch.

7

African elephant
(*Loxodonta africana*; Africa)

In spite of its tremendous weight, the elephant walks on the tips of its toes. Its foot is huge—over 12 inches wide—but the heel bone is raised off the ground, and the whole foot is cushioned with layers of fat—which is why the elephant treads so quietly even though it is so heavy.

Elephants eat about 300 pounds of plants, branches, and bark each day. Unlike other herbivores, or plant-eaters, they can't reach the ground with their mouths because their necks are so short. Instead, they use their incredible trunks to pluck leaves and squirt water into their mouths.

When food and water are in short supply, tusks are handy for digging holes in dry riverbeds and prying the bark off trees to get at the soft growth underneath. Tusks are actually super-long "incisor" teeth that wear away as the elephant grows older. Since each elephant uses one tusk more than the other, you can tell by the tusks whether an elephant is "right-handed" or "left-handed."

Bald eagle

(*Haliaeetus leucocephalus*;
North America)

The bald eagle is perfectly designed for high-altitude flying and high-speed hunting. Each of its wings is broad and nearly 4 feet long, so the eagle can glide for hours without flapping, or swoop down on its prey at more than 100 miles per hour.

Like all birds, the eagle has many thin, hollow bones, with bony struts, or braces, inside to make them strong yet lightweight. The breastbone, or sternum, has a large, thin "keel" to which the powerful flight muscles are attached. Large eye sockets house large, forward-facing eyes, which are typical of animals that hunt by sight. An eagle's vision is seven times sharper than yours!

Masai ostrich

(*Struthio camelus massaicus*; Africa)

Ostriches can't fly. Because they are so large, their bones are large too, and their wings are too small to lift their heavy bodies off the ground. But they can kick powerfully with their long, strong legs, and they can run nearly 35 miles per hour, outracing many flying birds and most other animals too. When they run, they often use their wings like sails and rudders, raising one and lowering the other to help them steer, or lifting both wings to brake.

Birds have more neck bones than other backboned animals, and ostriches have especially long, flexible necks. The head and beak can turn in all directions and do the jobs that hands would do, such as picking up food and cleaning feathers.

Blue whale

(*Balaenoptera musculus*;
worldwide)

Animals that live in the water can grow to a much more massive size than land animals because the water supports their weight. The blue whale, largest animal on earth, can weigh up to 150 tons. Its skeleton alone weighs 25 tons. A human skeleton weighs about 20 *pounds*.

The blue whale looks like a fish and lives in the water like a fish, but it is really a mammal, like you, and its skeleton is built a lot like yours. The bones in its flippers are similar to the bones in your hand, with four fingers rather than five—but each finger has extra bones which make the flipper much longer. Powerful up-and-down strokes of the whale's horizontal tail, or fluke, propel the animal through the water at nearly 30 miles per hour.

The small bones "floating" in the middle (only one is visible here) are the remains of the hipbones some types of whale once had.

The blue whale doesn't need arms and legs to chase and catch its food. It simply cruises into a school of tiny shrimplike creatures called krill, opens its enormous mouth, and swallows as many krill as it can—sometimes 10 tons in one meal!

12

Greater horseshoe bat

(*Rhinolophus ferrumequinum*; Europe, Asia, Africa)

Bats are the only mammals that can fly. Like birds, they have straw-thin, lightweight bones. But unlike birds, whose wings are made of feathers, bats' wings are made of skin. The skin is stretched over the arms, legs, and four extremely long finger bones. In fact, the bat flies with its fingers! It uses a clawlike thumb at the top of each wing for climbing up trees and across the ceilings of caves.

Most bats do not flap their wings from top to bottom the way birds do. Instead, they turn their wings in a rowing motion, like a swimmer doing the butterfly stroke. This movement is permitted by a complex "ball-and-socket joint" in the bat's shoulder.

Horseshoe bats are excellent flyers but clumsy walkers. Like all bats, they have knees that bend to the side (rather than forward, like human knees), so they can't move well on all fours—they are much too bowlegged!

14

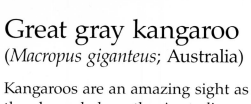

Great gray kangaroo
(*Macropus giganteus*; Australia)

Kangaroos are an amazing sight as they bound along the Australian grassland. Their Z-shaped legs and exceptionally long feet are typical of frogs, rabbits, and other animals that jump. They have to move fast out in the open, to escape from the wild dogs and human hunters who prey on them. With their huge, powerful hind legs, kangaroos can jump 40 feet in one leap.

The kangaroo's muscular tail is almost as long as the rest of its body. When kangaroos leap, they keep their balance by curving the tail up slightly behind them. When two rivals "box" with each other, they stand upright and put all their weight on the tail—which leaves the hind feet free for kicking.

15

Chinook salmon
(*Oncorhynchus tschawytscha*; North America, Asia)

Salmon are famous for their ability to journey hundreds of miles against the current and return to the same stream they were born in, where they mate and then usually die of exhaustion. A salmon can leap 10 feet in the air to hurdle waterfalls and other obstacles in its upstream drive.

With its hundreds of bones, the skeleton of a fish is more complicated than that of any other backboned animal, but it is made up of just three main parts: the skull, the backbone and ribs, and the fin skeleton— dozens of bones and rods which form the fins and tail.

Fish move by swinging the tail from side to side—not up and down like a whale—which drives them forward in the water. Unlike land animals, they can't grip the ground in order to turn or stop. Side fins help them steer, and fins on the back and belly keep them balanced so they won't roll over while swimming.

Painted turtle
(Chrysemys picta; North America)

A turtle can't fly or run from its enemies, but it can do something no other animal can do—pull its head, legs, and tail quickly into its shell and wait for the danger to pass.

The shell surrounds the turtle's body like a suit of armor and is actually part of the skeleton. The top shell, called the carapace, is made of an outside layer of horny scales and an inside layer of bone. The backbone and large, flattened ribs are fused, or joined, to the inside of the shell. A turtle could no sooner crawl out of its shell than you could crawl out of your skin.

The painted turtle, which spends most of its life in the water, is a strong swimmer. With its long, webbed back feet, it can paddle fast enough to catch a small fish. Like all turtles alive today, it has no teeth. It uses its pointed, beak-shaped jaws to tear its food into bite-size pieces.

House cat
(*Felis domestica*; worldwide,
except extreme polar regions)

A cat's front limbs lie closer to the
center of the chest than your front
"limbs," or arms. So cats can place
each foot precisely in front of the
other as they walk, enabling them to
glide along the top of a narrow fence
like a tightrope walker and not fall off.

When they do fall—even upside
down—they usually land on all fours.
This ability, called the righting reflex,
works particularly well in cats because
their backbones are so supple. The
reflex happens in a split second, but if
you could watch it in slow motion,
you would see the cat twist toward
the ground in stages—the head always
turns first, then the upper body, and
finally the rear. The stiffened tail
rotates the whole time like a propeller,
for balance, until the cat lands safely
on its feet with its back arched to
cushion the shock.

Cheetah

(Acinonyx jubatus; Africa)

The cheetah runs faster over short distances than any other animal, reaching 70 miles per hour in just 3 seconds. Cheetahs are champion sprinters because their bodies are built for speed. They are slender and streamlined, with a short skull and long, powerful legs. The backbone bends and then extends like a spring to propel the cheetah on its way. The tail is held straight out for balance.

The front legs don't rotate as much as yours do, so cheetahs don't slip and slide as their prey tries to dodge them.

Cheetahs are the only cats whose claws do not completely retract, or withdraw, into the paws, so the claws can dig into the ground for extra traction like the cleats on a baseball shoe. And like all cats, cheetahs walk on their toes, which lengthens their stride and enables them to run faster.

King cobra

(*Ophiophagus hannah*; western India, Southeast Asia, southern China)

Snakes have no arms, legs, or hands. They are all backbone, ribs, and muscle. The muscles are attached to each rib, and the snake moves by pushing the muscles against the ground or a nearby rock or plant, starting near the head and working back toward the tail. This rippling motion pulls the snake forward, and its scales give it a better grip on the surface.

The king cobra is especially agile, and its "threat posture" is well known. When in danger, it rises up and spreads its long, thin neck ribs, tightening the loose skin into a terrifying hood and making the snake look even bigger. It can sway like this for several minutes, and it is the only cobra that can actually move forward while in this position.

Cobras are carnivores, or meat-eaters, and like all snakes, they do not chew their food. Short, stiff fangs in the upper jaw act like hypodermic needles to inject venom, or poison, and stun the prey. The cobra then uses its jaws to "walk" the prey down its throat, swallowing it whole! The jaws are loosely connected to the skull, so the cobra can open its mouth extra wide. The left and right sides of the jaws are not joined solidly in the front, as yours are. They move independently to pull the prey toward the stomach, working the way your arms do when you haul on a rope.

Reticulated giraffe

(*Giraffa camelopardalis reticulata*;
Africa)

Much of the giraffe's awesome height is in its legs, which are like 6-foot stilts. The front legs are a little longer than the rear legs, so the giraffe has trouble reaching down and drinking from a water hole. To drink, the giraffe spreads its front legs far apart so that its shoulders are lower and its head can reach the ground.

The giraffe's neck is even longer than its legs, but it has only seven neck bones—the same number as you. Each of the giraffe's neck bones, however, is 10 inches high! With its long neck, a giraffe can feed on leaves that are beyond the reach of other animals.